About the Author

LIEUTENANT-GENERAL Sir John Glubb, KCB, CMG, DSO, OBE, MC, was celebrated as Chief of General Staff, The Arab Legion, a post he held from 1939 to 1956. He was the author of many books on Arab history and culture and on Middle East affairs.

This monograph is a transcript of a lecture delivered to the Institute for Cultural Research on 27 March, 1971.

MY YEARS
WITH THE ARABS

General Sir John Glubb

1971

MONOGRAPH SERIES NO. 8

The Institute for Cultural Research

My Years
with the Arabs

ANYONE WHO writes or speaks about Arabs is obliged, first of all, to say what he means by the word – who, in his opinion, the Arabs are. This introduction involves a little history. Basically, of course, the Arabs were the people who lived in the peninsula of Arabia, an area which today includes Saudi Arabia, the west side of the Persian Gulf, Oman and South Arabia and the Yemen. As most of the inhabitants of this area were nomadic, the word Arab also came to have the secondary meaning of nomads.

Let us begin our brief historical review in the seventh century AD. The world (omitting India and China) was at that time divided between an Eastern and a Western Power Bloc, as it has been for the past fifty years. The Eastern Power in the seventh century was Persia, the Western was the Roman Empire. Six hundred years after Christ, the countries which we call Turkey, Syria, Lebanon, Palestine, Egypt and Algeria had been Greek and Roman for nearly one thousand years. Syria and Egypt were more wealthy, cultured and important provinces in the Roman Empire than were France or Britain.

Iraq, on the other hand, had been part of Persia for a thousand years. In fact, in 600 AD, the capital of the Persian Empire was in Iraq, on the Tigris not far below Baghdad. The frontier between Rome and Persia ran approximately along the present border between Syria and Iraq.

The Arabs lived in Arabia, most of them were nomadic, and they were in contact with both Power Blocs, with Persia along the Euphrates, with Rome along the eastern borders of Syria.

The Prophet Muhammad began to preach in Mecca, in the Arabian Peninsula, in 613 AD and he died in 632. A year after his death, his enthusiastic followers burst out of their deserts and within eighty years conquered an empire extending from Spain and Morocco in the West, to India and the borders of China (in Central Asia north of the Pamirs) in the East.

Now the point which affects us is this. The population of Arabia, most of which is desert, is very small. Even today, the whole peninsula contains only about half the number of people as live in the Nile Delta alone. In the seventh century, most of these vast areas were conquered by little Arab armies of fifteen or twenty thousand men. Egypt, with a population of seven million, was occupied by an Arab force of about sixteen thousand men.

It has been estimated that, when all the conquests were over, only about one per cent of the inhabitants of the immense Arab Empire were of Arab descent, or had ancestors who had come from the Peninsula. The statements one sometimes reads to the effect that the Arabs 'poured' into Syria, Palestine or Egypt and that, henceforward, the inhabitants of all these countries were Arabs, are mathematically impossible. Moreover, the Arab conquests were not accompanied by massacres, evictions or exile. The original inhabitants remained unchanged.

Eventually, the majority of conquered peoples accepted the Muslim religion and the Arabic language. We may say, therefore, that the countries which we call Arab today share, to a great extent, the same religion, culture and language, but differ widely from one another in their ethnic origin. These racial differences cause them to react in entirely different ways to the events and the crises of life.

I think that the closest comparison we can make to them is South America, where everyone speaks Spanish (or Portuguese), everyone is Roman Catholic, but hardly any of them are Spaniards. In both cases, the situation is due to military conquest many centuries ago.

Personally, I served in Iraq and Jordan, and I had some experience of Saudi Arabians, Palestinians, Syrians and Lebanese. All these peoples differed widely from one another. Syria, Lebanon and Palestine form a narrow causeway connecting Asia and eastern Europe, on the one hand, with Africa on the other. Since the dawn of history, these countries have been endlessly invaded from the north and the south, from the desert and by sea across the Mediterranean. Hittites, Hurrians, Philistines from the Aegean, Greeks, Romans, Arabs, Turks, Armenians and many more have added to their racial composition.

No one, on the other hand, ever wanted to settle in Arabia, until the oil-rush in the 1940s. Syria is perhaps the most invaded country in history, Arabia the least such. Not only all races but all individuals are different from one another. There can be no easy and superficial generalisations for those who wish to understand. Human relations are extremely involved, and the sooner we reject sweeping generalisations and try to understand, the better we shall get on.

Courtesy

I do not want today to speak of battles or of political crises, but to try and tell you some of the things I learned in my thirty-six years with the Arabs. When I went out there in 1920, there were virtually no Europeans outside the big cities. Also, there was no BBC. Not that I wish to say anything against the BBC, but now that broadcasting exists, British people in Asia can daily recover the atmosphere of England.

They live, as it were, looking over their shoulders, counting the days till they can go home. This makes it much more difficult to lose yourself whole-heartedly in the country where you are. I was peculiarly lucky to arrive among the Arabs, when communication with home was extremely difficult. Such a situation may perhaps never recur.

What then did I learn? Firstly, two qualities which some may nowadays think unimportant – courtesy and dignity. Courtesy makes all human relations pleasant and easy. It is extremely practical also. Whether you are engaged on high diplomacy or buying a loaf of bread, courtesy will secure you better terms. For some reason, rudeness among us is considered democratic. The idea is erroneous. To be polite is not to be servile, indeed it is quite the opposite, if we are polite to rich and poor alike.

There are two different types of

courtesy in the Middle East, which we may generally speaking call 'city' and 'Arabian'. The Syrians seem to me to be the most courteous people I have ever known. Their politeness may be outward ritual, but it makes life easier all the same. Some say that they learnt the forms from the Byzantines, or from some much earlier period. When you are entering a doorway, you stand back and invite the other man to go first. When coffee comes round, you ask the coffee man to give a cup to someone else before you. If someone calls at your house, you say what an honour he has done you – and innumerable other little courtesies of the same kind.

The second form of courtesy is native to Arabia and has not been learned from foreign invaders. I remember once an American journalist asking if he could accompany me when I went for a drive in a car. We stopped at a small group of ragged tents in the desert and were invited in for coffee. A few rather threadbare carpets were spread and we sat down.

Seeing visitors, the men from other tents dropped in for coffee and the news. As each walked up to the tent, the other occupants all stood up and offered their seats to the newcomer, as they always do. When we were back in the car and driving on, the journalist burst out, 'Say, that has changed my views of life. I would not have believed that such poor people could be so courteous!' I have always remembered this remark, with its unconscious self-revelation of the attitude that the only 'nice' people are those who have money. This native Arabian courtesy characterises their relations among themselves. The early explorers called them 'nature's gentlemen', but nowadays we despise them because they do not have money.

In all Arab countries, today there are two cultures:

(1) Traditional forms of living and of human relationships.

(2) The 'educated' minority, whose principal aim is to imitate Western customs.

The ways of life to which I shall refer in the rest of this paper are of the old and traditional culture.

Dignity

I said that I had learned from the Arabs not only courtesy but dignity, a quality which is basic to all Middle East cultures. One is often ashamed of

Western visitors in the company of the local people. No Arab will lounge back in his chair, stick out his legs, yawn or roar with laughter with mouth wide open, unless it be in the absolute bosom of his family. In company, he will sit up straight, talk in a normal voice and never be loud or conspicuous. Europeans or Americans, scantily clad, who lounge around, shouting and making a noise, seem barbarians to these dignified people.

Western people, at least the more educated, used of course to obey much the same code of manners as people in the Middle East do now. It is presumably the wealth produced by the industrial revolution in the last two hundred years, which has changed the social behaviour of the West.

Religion

To the casual visitor, Arabs do not normally seem very pious. (Those who are trying to impress you with their modernity and Westernisation may tell you that they are atheists.)

Muslims are required to pray five times a day, wherever they may be. Many do not do so. Modern ways of life sometimes make it difficult. The prayers are supposed to be preceded by washing the hands, face and feet, but this is difficult to do for, for example, office workers or factory workers. It is complicated for people wearing European dress, to take off their socks and shoes. I must admit that I often met men who excused themselves from praying at the set times, owing to the impossibility of performing their ablutions. Few consider that it would be better to pray unwashed, than not to pray at all.

Incidentally, these five daily prayers are not really prayers at all, but little services of praise. There is a different word in Arabic for petitions to God. All the verses and prayers repeated five times a day are glorification of God.

Whether or not they perform all the rites exactly, it is still possible to say that all Arabs (except a few completely Westernised) believe in God. They accept His existence and the fact that He is almighty and All-Merciful. Perhaps it is illogical to believe completely in God and yet to lead a life not solely dedicated to Him, but most men do that of whatever religion they may be.

Among traditional Arabs, God is always present and always on their lips. Any reference to the future is always qualified by the phrase, 'If God wills'. Any enquiry regarding health, status, business conditions and so on, receives the reply 'God be praised'. When saying goodbye to someone going away, you say 'In God's safe keeping'. When your friend tells you he has opened a new business or bought some land, you say 'May God give you success'. If you yourself are setting out to go somewhere, you do not say, 'It is time to start', or 'Let's go', but 'Let's put our trust in God'.

Some of these phrases are conventional and do not mean very much, but I cannot help feeling that this continual mention of God does produce a stabilising effect on their characters.

An implicit belief in the existence of God certainly seems to provide a secure background for life. There are, for example, no suicides among these people. One of the commonest sneers directed against Muslims is that of fatalism. We are asked to think of them sitting inert waiting for fate to decide their lot. This charge seems to me completely misleading. They are as active as we are in pursuing their own affairs or defending their own interests.

The only foundation of which I can think for this charge of fatalism is that they accept their defeats and set-backs calmly. Instead of despairing or shooting themselves, they shrug their shoulders and say that such was God's will. It is a form of acquiescence to the inevitable. When the worst has happened, they do not rage against God and man. They say 'Praise to God; He wanted it that way', and resume their normal activities.

I cannot help feeling that most of our mental breakdowns and suicides are due to our loss of belief in the existence of God. Dr Jung, the great psychologist, is alleged to have said that the principal need of most of his mental patients was a firm religious faith.

Of course, we like to attribute the constant increase of nervous breakdowns and mental illness to 'the stress of modern life'. But I cannot help feeling that Arabs often live under greater stress than we. For example, the Palestine refugees, driven from their homes and their country by military force, and left to wander homeless and penniless year after year.

In the poorer parts of the Middle East, in the years when the rains fail, I have seen children picking individual undigested grains of barley out of horse and camel dung lying on the road. Tuberculosis is also terribly widespread among the poor and I have seen anguishing little families, the mother obviously coughing herself to death, with three or four children around her breathing in the disease. Yet there are no nervous breakdowns or suicides.

I cannot help feeling that it is their basic faith in the existence of God, which makes them bear such terrible misfortunes and hardships. When we deny God, we have no remaining object in going on living. A materialist who loses his material wealth has nothing to hope for or live for.

Money

Most of the traditional Arabs among whom I lived presented a phenomenon entirely strange, perhaps incredible, to the modern Western mind – they did not live for money.

Of course, like all of us, they needed money to live, but the accumulation of money was not important to them. This is not intended as a criticism of people in the West – our civilisation has developed in a manner which compels us to attach importance to money, and we live in fear of losing it and being left destitute. This situation, however, is also partly due in the West to the break-up of the family. Old people are not cared for and loved by their children, but are often thrust into some public institution, leaving the young to live as they wish without 'encumbrances', until they, in their turn, grow old and are pushed into a 'home' of some kind.

Among Arabs, such things cannot happen. The family automatically undertakes responsibility for all its members, and ageing people need not fear poverty or loneliness, and thus do not feel the constant struggle to accumulate money. I remember an old man saying to me, 'Money is like dirt on your hands. One day it's there and the next it is gone.' He was sitting cross-legged on the ground, boiling up a pot of coffee, on a little fire of twigs. He shrugged his shoulders philosophically – why worry about money?

One advantage of this lack of interest in money is that the poor are not jealous of the rich, as they are in the West. In general, Arabs are jealous people but not about money.

Lack of appreciation of this factor has led the Western Powers, particularly the United States, into innumerable errors. After the Second World War, American policy seemed to be largely based on the belief that the people of Asia only wanted money. 'Give them a higher standard of living and they will be quite happy', was the idea. This prescription, which was drawn up without examining the patient, was based on an entirely wrong diagnosis.

Of course, money is useful but not in return for a loss of dignity. The Western Powers themselves decided (quite sincerely in many cases) what the people of Asia needed, but they did not take much trouble to consult them, because they were 'backward peoples'. But when the money came, together with instructions as to how it should be used, it was often rejected. The West then denounced the Asians as being ungrateful. It was a sad misunderstanding.

Their unwillingness to put money first is described in the West as 'Oriental lethargy'. To most Western minds, making money is thought to be the basic human activity. They unconsciously assume that Asians hold the same view. The fact that they do not pursue this activity with all their energy is interpreted to be due to feebleness and lack of intelligence. No one in the West could visualise that there may be intelligent, strong and active people, who do not consider money-making as the purpose of human life.

Unfortunately our ideas are gaining ground. The many Asian students who graduate in Western universities carry home with them the news that the object of human life is to make money. They are partly persuaded to this view by the contempt of Western nations for poor countries. It is unpleasant to be treated as an inferior, and Arabs who mix for several years with the Western peoples, wish to introduce money-making, socialism, slack sexual morals and other Western customs of today, in order to escape from the slur of inferiority. Perhaps such influences will prove superficial and eventually fade.

When I first went to Jordan in 1930, there were no great differences in wealth, social classes or standards of living. Farmers and stockbreeders who borrowed money from merchants gave no receipts. Everyone trusted everyone else. I was interested in the indebtedness of the rural population and I often asked a nomad tribesman how much he owed to a merchant. As often as not the answer was, 'I don't know. Ask him.'

But all this has changed since Western laws and judicial procedure have been introduced. Merchants will no longer lend to a farmer without a legal document and a mortgage on the farm. If the rains fail in two consecutive years, the merchant forecloses on the mortgage and the farm becomes his property. He does not take it over, he leaves the farmer there. But henceforward the farmer pays a crippling 'rent' to the merchant for what was his own farm. The merchant grows rich and sends his son to a university in the United States. The farmer becomes a wage-slave on his own land.

When the sons return from America, they are 'educated'. They now form a superior class which looks down with contempt on the serfs who work on the land, whereas the grandfathers of both had been equals.

Western society today bitterly criticises in its own countries the gap in income between rich and poor, and the separation between social classes. Yet the Arabs, before the West came to them, were largely a classless society, with only a small gap between rich and poor. As a result of the introduction of Western ideas, the rich have grown richer and the poor poorer, and class distinctions have divided the people.

It is, of course, true that, in large cities, like Damascus, Aleppo and Baghdad there always were rich businessmen. But over the greater part of these countries there was far more social and financial equality than there is now.

Children

Under traditional Arab conditions, children grew up naturally in their families. In most cases, they continued in the family way of life, whether they were shepherds, farmers, merchants or whatever they might be. There was no caste system nor were there different social classes, but to follow on with the family occupation came naturally.

In towns, the boys went to day school and the girls learned domestic duties in their families. There were no clever people about, telling them that their parents were not handling them correctly and suggesting other ways of life. For all practical purposes, the boys served their apprenticeships in their families, it being understood that 'family' did not mean father and mother and the children, but a wide circle of aunts, uncles, grandparents, cousins and more distant connections and neighbours.

Living among such a cross-section of the community, amid people of every age from babies to grandmothers, no one had ever heard of a 'generation gap', a sickness gratuitously invented by us in the last thirty years.

We collect thousands of young people together in colleges or universities, cut off from family contacts. In the United States, there are universities of thirty-five thousand or more students. I taught for one term at such an institution. I was accommodated in a little house on the campus, but all the professors lived out, sometimes several miles away, and 'commuted' to the college every morning. At night, I was the only adult on the campus.

In the larger universities, the professors often did not know the names of their students, nor, in some cases, did the students know the names of the professors or the lecturers. There were few if any human relationships, and virtually no guidance, advice, consultation or personal contacts. Teaching became the cramming of the 'facts' into the students' memories. This left no scope for influence, for character building, for absorbing the wisdom or the philosophy of the professor.

Governments at the same time press the universities to increase their 'output' of students, just as they press factories to raise their output of cars, porcelain, electronics, lipstick or whatever it may be. University education becomes increasingly a production-line, mass-output problem. Students are fed in at one end, 'facts' are placed in their memories as they pass along the conveyor belts and, at the other end, they come out graduates.

Adolescents suffer from intense emotional problems, increased by the introduction of co-education. But their problems are by no means limited to sex. The object of life, the existence of God, the reform of society and a hundred other problems involve them in emotional and spiritual anxieties. For four or five years, at this most sensitive time of their lives, they are cut off from the natural, loving and essential advice and sympathy of mothers, fathers and relations. No wonder many become delinquents, drug-addicts, or suicides.

The other side of this tyrannical system is that academic degrees are considered the one essential to success. Character, honesty, experience, courage are never enquired of, or even thought necessary.

High academic qualifications are really necessary for only a small number of professions. A far greater number of occupations necd precisely those qualities which are never thought of and which cannot be academically taught, but only absorbed from other persons with whom we live, or acquired in the rough apprenticeship of life.

None of these problems arise in Arab society, except in a few places where universities have been formed which slavishly imitate Western methods. To those who have been fortunate enough to live intimately inside both Asian and Western communities, the situation seems ironical indeed. The three problems which today cause the most perplexity in the West seem to be the difference in incomes between the very rich and the very poor, the existence of social classes and the 'generation gap' between young and old. None of these problems existed in Arab society in general (excluding Egypt) before 1914. As the result of the spread of European ideas, all are now increasing in the Middle East.

Wisdom and Knowledge

One of the most striking peculiarities of life in this country, which has impressed me since my return to Britain, is the loss of our appreciation of the difference between Wisdom and Knowledge.

This development is doubtless due to the expansion of science in education, and to the general veering of the attitude of the general public towards what they believe to be science. In general, what we call science is the study of the material facts of this world. These facts can be ascertained and committed to memory. They are normally governed by laws, that is to say that certain processes may be trusted always to produce the same result.

Thus material science, like

mathematics, is the result of cause and effect and can be mastered with accuracy. A vast amount of 'knowledge' of these material phenomena has been accumulated and can be known. More knowledge of material facts is constantly being acquired and added to the store.

Wisdom is as different from knowledge as chalk is from cheese. It is an activity of an entirely different nature. Wisdom cannot be taught to a class nor learned from a textbook. It is the art of living and can only be acquired by experience gained in the process of living. While it is true that it cannot be taught in a set lesson, it can to some extent be 'caught' by living with another person or other persons, who are wise. But, really, to know how to live can only be ascertained by living.

Wisdom is thus an art which deals

with human beings, for the secret of happy and successful living lies in our relationship with other people. It is an atmosphere, an attitude, at times it almost seems like an aura.

Wisdom has no connection with acquired knowledge. An old peasant may be wiser than the world's greatest scientist. Sometimes, indeed, wisdom and knowledge seem to be incompatible. Great knowledge can often produce intellectual pride, and a contemptuous attitude towards 'uneducated' people. Humility is the essence of wisdom. Pride and arrogance are the very antithesis of wisdom.

I remember once calling on the Ameer Abdulla of Jordan. As I entered the ante-chamber, a number of politicians came out of the king's room. When I was shown in, he said to me, 'If I were to drive out into the desert, and stop and ask the first shepherd I met whether we should fight against the Jews in Palestine, he would ask me, "How many men have you got and how many have they?" Even a shepherd knows that there is no use fighting if you cannot win. But these politicians all have university degrees, they despise all of us who have not. Yet if I prove to them that we shall lose by starting a war, they reply that Zionism is unjust, we must fight. I agree as much as they do that it is unjust, but it is not wise to fight when the enemy is stronger'.[¶]

On one or two occasions I have remarked that I have known village

[¶] This occurred in 1948, just before the end of the British Mandate and before the Proclamation of Israel.

headmen in Asia, who were wiser than the President of the United States. I am regarded as a lunatic, yet there is nothing absurd in such a statement.

Sometimes I wonder whether a technological age is compatible with wisdom. In theory, of course, a physicist or a mathematician can be as wise as anyone else. But our occupations produce impalpable effects on our minds, of which we ourselves are entirely unaware. Certainly living in a constant hustle is incompatible with wisdom, which requires not only humility but a measure of detachment from the wild rush of modern city life. There is much truth in the saying that we have learnt how to control matter, but have lost the art of controlling men.

Politics

We are rightly proud of the fact that we no longer persecute people for their religious beliefs. But, in politics, we are as narrow as our ancestors were in religion. We are as small-minded, perhaps more so, than were our ancestors of several centuries ago.

Nobody, in any age or country, has found the ideal way of governing men. When we look around us today, with our strikes, our protests, our financial crises, our rising crime statistics, we can scarcely claim that we have found the perfect system. Yet we insist that everyone else in the world must adopt our methods.

Presumably the ideal of government is to find the correct balance between authority and freedom. The perfect method of achieving this end is for the people to love their rulers and, consequently, to obey their authority willingly without compulsion.

On one occasion during the Second World War, a foreign correspondent asked if he could tour Jordan. We gave him all the facilities he requested, but we did not give him an escort, who might have inhibited his conversations with the local people. He returned in a fortnight and the first thing he said was, 'This is the first country I have ever visited where everyone I have spoken to praises the government.'

Many years later, when I had left Jordan, I was being interviewed by a British journalist, who said to me, 'I assume you would agree that the government of Jordan in your time was entirely reactionary and feudalistic, and really an anachronism in the modern world.' A comparison between these two stories seems to me enlightening.

It may, perhaps, be admitted that Asian governments used to tend towards paternalism, a word rarely used in this country without a sneer. The relation of the government to the public was like that of a father to his children – one of affection and mutual understanding. Such systems were often extremely happy, as I know from experience. To be contented with the government is called in the West 'Asian lethargy'.

Living in England, we take our 'democracy' for granted without much thought, but coming to this country after thirty-six years in Asia, certain points impress one forcibly. One of those which I found most interesting was that our democracy always means strife. Europeans who came to Jordan, in the old happy days when everyone liked the government, would urge the people to form an opposition. A situation where everyone was happy was not democracy.

During the period of the Mandate in Palestine, the British Government gave orders that Trade Unions must be established. There were no industrial disputes, which was assumed to mean that somebody must be oppressing someone else. The Trade Unions remained in existence on paper until the British left, when no one ever heard of them again.

Presumably the Western assumption is that all men must seek their own interests, and consequently that the strong will always oppress and defraud the weak. The assumption is not correct. The most important thing about every organisation is not its laws or its constitution, but the spirit which inspires it. Spirit is not allowed for in a materialist system, which is chiefly interested in money.

In fact, however, under traditional paternalistic systems, a spirit of affection does often unite the ruler and the people thereby producing a happy country, until Western democracy arrives on the scene and sets every man against his neighbour.

This constant desire to provoke a quarrel is to me very curious. I was once giving a lecture in England, when somebody stood up and contradicted me. The chairman rubbed his hands with delight. 'This is fine,' he said. 'Now we can have a good row.'

In the United States, I have often been asked to engage in a public debate with someone thought to hold opposite views. The result of such public debates is usually that both sides go much further than they would otherwise have done. Moreover the audience gets angry also and both sides to the debate become much more violent and malevolent than before. We constantly lament the bitter hatreds with which we are surrounded, yet most of them have been introduced and stoked up to fever heat by ourselves.

Government

The Prophet Muhammad began life as a religious teacher, but gradually became the ruler of a community who depended solely on him. He found himself their administrator and their army commander. When he died, his successors sought only to imitate his example. Every successive Muslim regime was ruled by a single man, who was the religious, political and military head of the community.

In theory, the ruler must be the best available man for the post. In theory, also, the headship of the State was not hereditary, and quite often it was not so in fact. The ruler, when selected, was not supposed to surround himself with royal pomp and ritual. The early Arab Khalifs used to walk in the streets, rubbing shoulders with their fellow citizens.

Accessibility

The key to the traditional Arab form of government was accessibility. The ruler frequently, sometimes every day, sat in an open hall to which everybody was admitted. Anyone present could address him, explain his grievance and ask for redress. Sometimes a messenger was sent off immediately to bring the person against whom the complaint was made, and the affair was settled immediately. In any case, there were no lawyers, no legal fees and no avoidable delays. Everyone had direct access to the man who had the power to give a decision.

When the Arabs had conquered a great empire, it was, of course, no longer possible for the Khalif (Caliph) in person to hear every complaint. But the same system was reproduced on a smaller scale in every province, where the local governor would sit in public every day and hear complaints.

It may, of course, be admitted that so simple a system could no longer be applied in a complicated society like our own, with such immense numbers of laws which only professional lawyers can understand. Two points, however, are worth recording.

Firstly, that the Arabs did have a system of government, which was highly developed and produced and administered the largest empire the world had ever seen.

Secondly, that the basic principle of their system was that one man must be responsible for every job, and that he must be accessible to his public. If he proved unsatisfactory, he could be dismissed, or even murdered, and a better man appointed. But the Arab system made no allowance for government by assemblies, committees or other joint bodies.

By contrast, our own system today has completely lost the chief asset of the Arab system, namely accessibility. No single man is responsible for anything.

Information conveyed to complainants always takes the form that the council, the committee, the department, or whoever it might be, decided this or that.

In addition to the fact that, with us, the individual is always concealed in a committee, the immense and increasing amount of paper work with which all officials are flooded, makes it difficult for them to see, and listen to, people. The result is a dehumanised and depersonalised machine. In the Middle East, human relationships are of supreme importance. They cannot understand a depersonalised system conducted in official memoranda, or loyalties to vague ideas like socialism, capitalism or communism.

Personally, I think that different nations need different systems, many of which are based on traditions thousands of years old. If I criticise at all, it is the arrogance with which we assume that our particular system is the only one which should be followed by the whole human race. 'Western Democracy' may or may not be the best system for us. But no one has discovered the ideal system of government and many other forms exist, some of them with traditions much older than ours, and which operate successfully in the various countries where they originated.

I feel that we are not justified in demanding that all these other nations abandon their traditions and institutions and adopt our own.

Chivalry

There is one other point to which I should like to refer, because it has always appealed to me, even if it may not be thought important in the modern world. It is the origin of chivalry.

Before the preaching of Islam in the seventh century AD, the Arabs consisted largely of nomadic tribes, which lived in the desert, where they carried on endless wars against one another. These wars, however, were governed by strict rules of honour, and had virtually no political object – that is to say, no tribe wished to conquer, subdue or exterminate another tribe. Perhaps their basic cause was the need felt by the tribesmen for some excitement and glamour in their otherwise monotonous lives.

The object of their wars, therefore, was to provide a means by which men could win honour, rather than wealth or power. Thus to fight honourably was more important than to win. When men compete for honour, it is natural that women should be the arbiters of honour, and it is for their favour that men compete. This factor gave women an honourable status among the Bedouin tribes, which they did not enjoy in the cities or in the agricultural community.

It was these very nomads who formed the spearhead of the Arab conquests. The romanised populations of Syria and Egypt rejected these nomad customs and the Bedouins passed on with the wave of conquest, many of them finishing up in Spain or in Afghanistan.

In Spain and in the south of France they established their ideas of war for honour, and a chivalrous attitude towards women. It is not always remembered that the Arabs remained in Spain for nearly eight hundred years, a period as long as from Edward

III to ourselves. During the early centuries, first Normandy and then Southern France, belonged to the King of England. Thus France, Spain and England, the homes of European chivalry were all in close touch with the Arabs of Spain.

Dr Levi-Provencal, a great French scholar, is the best-known expert in our times on the subject of the Arabs in Spain. Many English people are surprised to read one of his statements to the effect that 'the Arabs taught Europe respect and courtesy to women'.

A list of all the monographs to be published in the series:

An Eye to the Future
Dr. Alexander King, Dr. Martin Holdgate, Eugene Grebenik, Dr. Kenneth Mellanby, George McRobie

East and West, Today and Yesterday
Sir Stephen Runciman, Patrick O'Donovan, Peter Brent, Sir Roger Stevens, Nirad C. Chaudhuri, Iris Butler, Prof. G.M. Carstairs, Richard Harris

Science and the Paranormal
Leonard Lewin, D.Sc.

Sufic Traces in Georgian Literature
Katharine Vivian

Rembrandt and Angels
Michael Rubinstein

Biological and Cultural Evolution
Mary Midgley

The Age of Anxiety: a Reassessment
Malcolm Lader

Goethe's Scientific Consciousnes
Henri Bortoft

The Healing Within: Medicine, Health and Wholeness
Robin Price

A Clash of Cultures: The Malaysian Experience
David Widdicombe, Q.C.

Evaluating Spiritual and Utopian Groups
Arthur J. Deikman, M.D.

Malta's Ancient Temples and Ruts
Rowland Parker & Michael Rubinstein

Cults in 19th Century Britain
Robert Cecil

Black Culture and Social Inequality in Colombia
Peter Wade

Urban Legends and the Japanese Tale
David Schaefer

The Role of 'Primitive' People in Identifying and
Approaching Human Problems
Contributed by Cultural Research Services

The Use of Omens, Magic and Sorcery for Power
and Hunting
Contributed by Cultural Research Services

Ritual from the Stone Age to the Present Day
Contributed by Cultural Research Services

Problem-solving and the Evolution of Human
Culture
Stephen Mithen

Cultural Identity: Solution or Problem?
Peter Wade

Inventions and Inventing: Finding Solutions to
Practical Problems
Kevin Byron

Problems, Myths and Stories
Doris Lessing

Modern Primitives: The Recurrent Ritual of
Adornment
Contributed by Cultural Research Services

Baptised Sultans: The contribution of Frederick II
of Sicily in the transfer and adaptation of
Oriental ideas to the West
Contributed by Cultural Research Services

Brain Development During Adolescence and Beyond
Dr. Sarah-Jayne Blakemore

Collective Behaviour and the Physics of Society
Philip Ball

Counter-Intuition
Dr. Kevin Byron

Music, Pleasure and the Brain
Dr. Harry Witchel

Fields of the Mind
Dr. Rupert Sheldrake

Why do we leave it so late?
David Canter

Scheherazade and the global mutation of
teaching stories
Robert Irwin

Consciousness, will and responsibility
Chris Frith

Extraordinary Voyages of the Panchatantra
Ramsay Wood

www.ingramcontent.com/pod-product-compliance
Lightning Source LLC
Chambersburg PA
CBHW020608030426
42337CB00013B/1267

* 9 7 8 1 7 8 4 7 9 8 8 5 7 *